DREAMS OF LIFE

MERVIN M. FRANCIS

Copyright © Mervin M. Francis 2025

Second edition

Cover Photograph by Chanel Pillay 2021
Cover Design by Sanjel Aaron Govender 2021

ISBN: 978-0-6398518-2-2

All rights reserved. This publication, and no part thereof may be reproduced in any form or by any means, electronic, mechanical, photocopying, recording, scanning, or otherwise without written permission from the publisher. It is against copyright law to copy this book, upload it to a website, or distribute it by any other means without the publisher's permission.

mervin@sakurabookpublishing.com

Dreams Of Life is dedicated to my loved ones, who continue to inspire me to chase my dreams; and to my family and friends, who support my work.

A special thanks to the Heavenly Father for bestowing upon me the amazing gift of poetry.

DREAMS OF BROTHERHOOD

My Bro
(In Loving Memory of Christopher)

I greet you every morning as I begin my day
I wish there was more to you I could say
I wish I could hear your voice, my bro
For I miss you dearly and only my heart would know

The years go by but your memories live on
You were young when Our Father called on you, his son
This world was just a place to meet
The times we shared were awesome and sweet.

Though many years have passed us by
I miss you each day and that is no lie
I know for sure that we will meet again
In the Heavens above, where there is no pain

I know that you are looking down on me
But only at my alter, your face shall I see
I am glad that I got to show you how much I cared
Thank you, God, for the times that we shared.

Brothers For Life

(Dedicated To My Toyota Brothers)

We met in a place where we knew no one
A place where our working lives had begun
As time passed us by, we learned more about each other
A friendship was forged under the term of brother

Brothers for life was what we chose to be
And our journey together set our relationship free
No matter the mood we made time to speak
And shared a drink after a hectic week

The weekend trips that we took together
They were times of enjoyment like no other
The fun that we had when we let down our hair
No offence to those whose heads are bare

I am proud to have known you guys all these years
Even those that climbed the heavenly stairs
I dare not change the way that we are
You are my brothers for life and we have come so far.

Strong Winds
(In Memory of Pradeep 'Nicky' Ramataur)

I closed my eyes and imagined what to do
I have to hit this ball with a swing so true
"Not too aggressive", I hear my thoughts say,
"The wind is strong, and it will be blown away."

I positioned myself and took a swing
I watched in awe as the wind did its thing
I know in my mind that I hit it with ease
But I failed to realize the strength of this breeze

I stood and watched as the ball took flight
Into the bushes, oh what a sad sight
My heart sank from what I just saw
Underestimating the strong winds was my greatest flaw

I managed to keep the next ball in play
I walked to the bush where the first one went astray
Hoping to find it so I can claim this victory
Only to watch my opponent smile and say, "Sorry."
Head dropped down, I found my ball
But played out to the green and watched him take it all.

DREAMS OF LIFELONG BONDS

A Special Friend

There is a space in my heart reserved for you
A space for this friendship, a space so true
For I trust the way you make things right
Even when you are out of sight

You never listen to what others say
Never judging me in any way
Positive thoughts are always shared
From a special friend that has always cared

I turn to you when times are tough
I listen to your words and that is enough
To help me clear my troubled mind
Only words of wisdom from you I find

Thank you, God, for this special friend
A treasure for me to keep till the end
As I look back at all life had to offer
You made me strong enough to never have to suffer.

I Found A Friend

I found a friend without searching for one
Her smile was warmer than the summer sun
She looked at me with inviting eyes
To stand beside her, oh what a surprise

She is a Godsend in my time of need
A friendship to not just flourish but also exceed
A friendship to nourish and nurture as time passes by
To lend a shoulder if ever she should cry

To stand beside me when times are tough
To steady the ship when seas get rough
I hope that this friendship stays forever strong
And I hope that for her, I do no wrong

To be there for each other through the good times and bad
To shower her with happiness whenever she is sad
I pray to be strong for I have found a friend
I pray for strength to keep this bond till the end.

My Friend

My thoughts go out to you my friend
I pray this pain will one day end
I pray for strength so you can stand up strong
I pray for wisdom to remain within you lifelong

I pray for brightness to light up your way
So that you will be loved come what may
I pray for this pain to leave your side
So that from happiness you need not hide

But most of all I pray you find peace
For the aching in your heart will one day cease
As your broken heart begins to mend
Remember you are never alone, my friend.

DREAMS OF BEAUTY

A Beautiful Star

Like a thief in the night you stole my sleep
Keeping me awake, I was lost too deep
How I hoped that you would stay in my mind
Or in my heart your warmth I would find

But it was only my dreams that made you feel real
Only in my dreams could your glances I steal
Your vision of beauty is captured on screen
A Goddess of the movies where we live for every scene

You are captured by the world of beauty my star
Living on the stage in a country so far
Adored and loved by millions out there
But only with one your heart can share
How blessed is he to hold you in his arms
How blessed indeed to receive all your charms.

A Maiden So Fair

A maiden so fair, a breath of fresh air
As she passed me by, I could only but stare
For her mere presence had left me breathless
Whilst my thoughts of her were purely endless

I wished I had the courage to speak
Or to take her in my arms and kiss her cheek
But I was scared for I felt that I was no match
I doubted that even her attention I could catch

For a vision of beauty is all that I saw
Strolling gracefully out the door
I gazed longingly as she walked away
Though she had left, with me her vision shall stay

I hoped for another encounter with her someday
I will cherish that moment, should it come my way
She was truly a vision of beauty to see
I pray that one day she will come to me.

Angel

This world was blessed when your mother gave birth
For an angel was sent from Heaven to Earth
A vision of beauty, a woman so kind
A woman with wisdom and a powerful mind

Her beauty was subtle, and she carried it true
Her heart was poured into everything she would do
Watching her perform although she is afar
How true it is that she was born to be a star

How spoilt we are to hear this angelic voice sing
For the joy to the world her songs do bring
A special thanks to the Father Above
For sending us an angel, to fill our hearts with love.

Brown Eyes

When I looked into those beautiful brown eyes
My heart skipped a beat and knew you were first prize
The way they looked back at me
Allowed my emotions to finally roam free

These strange feelings that had seemed to be lost
Had found its way back but at what cost?
What is happening to me if only I knew
For answers I search but I still have no clue

Why am I at a loss for the words to say?
Will it be here in my heart forever to stay?
For this feeling within is strange and new
And these feelings somehow feel so true

And as the day starts to slowly fade away
I wish for that moment forever to stay
Embedded in my mind, a dream so whole
It refreshes my mind, my heart and soul.

Fire Of Love

There is a fire that is about to start
Burning deep within my heart
This flame of love burns very bright
And the joy it brings cannot be hidden from sight

The smiles and happiness are endless and true
The feelings within make the sky turn blue
The beauty it bares is seen from afar
The glow from within shines like a Christmas star

Unlimited happiness it brings to us all
Pleasures and joy even if we fall
These amazing feelings we are blessed to share
From this fire of love, for this maiden so fair.

How Awesome A Sight

I watched as a smile danced across your face
My heart skipped a beat as your aura filled this place
How awesome a sight I got to share
Into those brown eyes I could simply only stare

I was captured by your looks and even that smile
Into my memory that moment I will forever file
This beauty that stands in front of me
Is she for real or is it a mirage that only I see?

I am known to dream even though I am awake
Please let it be real, for my heart will not handle the ache
I love what I see whilst I am standing here tall
May this moment be a treasure that I could daily recall.

I Close My Eyes

I close my eyes and try to sleep
But thoughts of you still run so deep
Now I am awake and thinking of you
Help me, please, for I know not what to do

As I lay alone and deep in thought
With visions of you that my mind has sought
What can I do to make my heart feel better?
Should I pen the words and write you a letter?

Would you be happy to hear how I feel?
Would you embrace me and make everything real?
Why do I feel that I am stuck in a dream?
Should I awaken so that my pride I may redeem?

I Could

I could send you flowers but they will wither and die
Even though their beauty might catch your eye
I could send you chocolates to sweeten up the deal
With hopes that your feelings, I am able to steal

I could make you breakfast to start up your day
Set you up with a smile before you go your way
I could be your lighthouse when you are lost at sea
With the relief that your safety is my guarantee

I could share with you my thoughts so deep
And all the happiness in the world will be yours to keep
I can give you a place in my heart
Hoping with you, it will not break apart.

I Was Captured

I was captured by that beautiful face
My mind had left me though I stood in place
What spell has this lady put me under?
For my heart was pounding yet filled with wonder

I felt the rush of blood to my head
Even though I lay flat, just in my bed
Thoughts of her flooded my mind
To any other sight, my eyes were blind

The only thing that I could see
Is the beautiful face that has captured me
What can I do to take back control?
To get back my mind and make me feel whole?
Her beauty was simply captivating
And from that feel I truly need saving.

My Eyes Are Sleeping

My eyes are sleeping but my heart is awake
These feelings for you I find hard to shake
What is wrong? For I cannot let you go
My heart is awake and I need you to know

The reason for this is glaring at me
My eyes may be asleep yet clearly, I see
The emotions within are hard to hide
It engulfs my thoughts like a rising tide

Should I shout it out for all to hear?
Or should I send it only to you out there?
Though my eyes are sleeping and my heart is awake
May love consume me whole and my sleep never break.

Shooting Star

I wished upon a shooting star
That you will remain as sweet as you are
I dare not want you to change your ways
Although we have so many lonely days.

There will come a time when we will be together
And from then on, you will need not bother
For harder times will have passed us by
And we will still be together, withstanding time

Our love will be the bond that keeps us strong
And together forever is where we both belong
The time will come when you will see
Just how much you really mean to me.

You are so rare, you could be from another realm
To me you are a precious gem
I trust our love to show us a beautiful path
That we can travel within our heart.

Sweet Words

I hear your voice, I hear your band
Far across the distant land
The music I hear takes me back in time
When unexpected heights my heart would climb

Your music leaves my mind out of control
Whilst your sweet words capture my soul
When I close my eyes, I am lost in your song
And I cannot stop myself from singing along

How sweet are the sounds that reach my ears
The depth of your emotions wipes away all fears
A smile shared with you in a stolen glance
Gives me the confidence to rise slowly and dance
Your music moves me with so much ease
That lost in your voice I am in heavenly peace.

The First Time I Saw You

The first time I saw you, I was in awe
This vision of beauty knocked me to the floor
My heart was racing and I was unsure of what to do
Whilst this Angel left me breathless and blue

The wind was taken out of my sail
And from my lips words simply did fail
To explain how I felt was no simple task
And I had no answers if someone were to ask

The first time I saw you, oh what a sight
To not drop down on one knee took all my might
I tried to walk but could not move
For my heart was dancing to a brand-new groove

It took me a while to get back in control
I turned my gaze and took a stroll
Avoided the chance to get caught in her sight
Deciding that I will sit back until the time was right.

This Vision Of Beauty

This vision of beauty, this lady so fair
I can spend my hours, just caressing her hair
Her heart is so pure and filled with love
Her voice floats gracefully on the wings of a dove

If only she knew of these feelings within me
Would she approve of what she will see?
Do I dare to ask her what she thinks?
Or avoid it in the fear that my heart might sink?

If only the joy from my heart could be free
I would hold her in my arms, close to me
This vision of beauty standing by the stream
Glances my way just as I begin to awake from
my beautiful dream.

When I Look Back

When I look back at the times that we had
I remember that not all of them were bad
Though we fought and argued a lot
I could not forget how much joy the good times brought

There never was a dull moment that we got to share
Even those times playing truth or dare
The silence together also brought a lot of happy times
Whilst we just laid there listening to the soundless nights

Whilst time passes us by, and we think of those days
Joy fills my heart where forever it stays
Your memories I will cherish for all the days to come
And of the moments in time I know where they are from

For me to move forward, I must look back
On happier times when our love was on track
Joy and happiness were always around
And never a dull moment was ever to be found.

Would You Be Bold?

Would you be bold enough to talk to me?
Or even be ready to set your heart free?
Would you be strong enough to take up the fight?
Or allow your emotions to soar to new height?

Would you be able to share how you feel?
So that together our emotions would always be real
Would you dare to hold me in your arms?
And add warmth to my heart with all of your charms

Would you be ready to join me on a ride?
Throw caution to the wind and choose not to hide?
Would you be ready to set your heart free?
And spend the rest of your life with me?

DREAMS OF THE HEART

A Message

A message from a loved one rings quite clear
As it comes from the heart, without any fear
With words filled with truth and sincerity
With promises to be shared for an eternity

These messages from the heart are always true
Whilst it often leads to a point of lovers saying,
"I do"
With a promise to lead a lifetime of happiness together
A message to stand firm always and forever

Take head to the message that comes from the heart
Treasure and nurture it right from the start
It strengthens the bonds of true love
With the strength of a seal sent from the Heavens above.

A Vision

A vision of beauty captured by the moonlight
A lady whose heart shines ever so bright
She teases my thoughts with her love
As pure and graceful as the Heavens above

If only she knew what she has done to me
My heart has been captured and is no longer free
What can I do to show her how I feel?
How can I help her so that her heart might heal?

When times are tough and words are few
I will always be here for her, if only she knew
Such is the way of the life that we bear
Unspoken thoughts become a silent prayer
If only these hearts collided in the past
I would be living the dream and making it last

But life is not a straight road that we take
It is littered with all the mistakes that we make
So embrace the time that you get today
And hold on to the memories forever I pray.

Beautiful Eyes

When I look into those beautiful eyes
How I wonder about the truth and lies
Tears of sorrow and tears of joy
Tears you have shed for a silly old boy.

Filled with joy they look so fine
How blessed am I to see them shine
As time passes by without a care
May that sparkle forever stay there

Keep them open to the beauty around
Taking in the sky with your feet planted firmly
on the ground
Enjoy the magic that you get to see
And may those beautiful eyes forever roam free.

By My Side

I feel all strange deep inside
These feelings for you I will never hide
Know that this love I have for you
Is special, sweet, tender, and true.

It gives me the greatest strength and hope
And with any problems I find it easier to cope
Just knowing that you are there by my side
And one day for sure you will be my bride.

Until that special day comes along
To you my heart will always belong
And all that I ask of you to do
Is return my love and keep it true.

From this bond that we both share
Our hearts will forever have tender love and care
And with all the pleasure that our love will bring
Our hearts forever with joy shall sing.

Close Your Eyes

Close your eyes and tell me what you see
Close your eyes and search your heart for me
Think of the moments when we are apart
Tell me beautiful, what lies in your heart?

Close your eyes and search your mind
Close your eyes and tell me what you find
Are there thoughts of us that make you smile?
Are there thoughts that make you want to stay a while?

Close your eyes and tell me what you see
Close your eyes and set your emotions free
Free to complete this love so rare
So rare that nothing in this world can compare

Close your eyes and search for me
Close your eyes and set your heart free
Free to allow you to embrace our love
Free to show you that it is blessed from above

Don't Cry

Hush my Angel and don't you cry
For my love for you can be no lie
Look into my eyes and tell me what you see
Yes, a vision of beauty roaming ever so carefree.

That vision of you lurks deep in my heart
Embedded forever, till death do us part
The time spent with you is captured up above
For they are treasured memories filled only with love.

So, whenever you are alone or thinking of me
Remember, for you my heart forever will be
Hush my Angel and don't you cry
For I love you truly and that is no lie.

Fire Within

In the depths of my heart burns a raging fire
For the yearning of life, I will never tire
You are the flame that burns so bright
You are my beginning, my end and my guiding light

You give me the strength to stand up tall
You hold me up when I begin to fall
Your love is the anchor that keeps me grounded
Your love is my solace when I feel surrounded

How blessed am I to have you here
How blessed that our future seems so clear
The fire within breathes life and love
This special bond is a blessing from above

Never lose faith in all that you do
Always have hope in a love so true
Always show the world what you are all about
And never allow for the fire within to go out.

Heartbeat

I felt your heartbeat as I held you tight
I felt your warmth throughout the lonely night
I saw tears in your eyes as you awoke
I felt the pain in your voice as you spoke

If only there was a way to take away your pain
To return joy to the heart that has taken such strain
To fill you with hope and mend the heart that was broken
To change your thoughts of certain words that were spoken

These words that play over in your mind
These words an eraser I hope I would find
These words that seemed to have destroyed your love forever
A cure for this pain I hope I could deliver

To allow your heart to be free once more
To gain the confidence to pick yourself off the floor
I hope that time will heal your mind
I trust that love one day you will find.

Hearts Dreams

All my dreams are built around you
My love for you will forever be true
I know not what the future will bring
But I know I will do my best to make your heart sing.

Sacred are the dreams that comes from the heart
And nothing on Earth can tear them apart
For love is the king that rules this throne
And such is my heart that could never turn to stone

There comes a time when we all must learn
To stem the tide and allow your dreams to burn
For they are fueled by love and happiness
A thing so powerful and filled with greatness
It guides our hearts, as well as our lives
It gives us the courage to help us thrive.

I Will

I will hold you gently in my arms
I will protect you from all harm
I will stroke your hair as it falls on your face
I will love you so, for my all days

I will speak words of comfort when you feel alone
I will be right beside you when you face the unknown
I will turn your darkness into light
I will protect you from the dangers of the night

I will listen for as long as you wish to speak
I will lift up your spirit when things seem bleak
I will remind you always of this bond that treasure
I will love you endlessly, forever and ever.

I Wish
(In Loving Memory of Sandra Matilda Naicker)

I felt your kisses upon my face
I felt your joy fill up this place
I searched for you deep in my heart
I searched for you, near and apart

I wish that you were close to hold me tight
I wish that you were never out of my sight
I stare up at the Heavens, if only for a while
Wishing I was blessed once again to see your smile

These things from you that my heart wishes for
Make them come true, just walk through that door
Take me in your arms and kiss away every fear
Hold me tight and say that you are near

When times are tough, and I feel all alone
Your memories begin to melt this heart of stone
The treasures of our bond burn bright through the pain
And as always, my wish is all that shall remain.

Life Is A Journey

Life is a journey so enjoy the ride
But a journey is better with a partner by your side
To keep you company on a road so long
To make you feel better when things go wrong

To correct you when you stray off the path
And to support you in everything, right from the start
So when the road starts to reach a bend
Go with the flow and ride it to the end

The journey of life is not always straight
It has many twists that you may come to hate
So always put faith in the one by your side
Hold on tight and enjoy the ride.

Like A Thief In The Night

Like a thief in the night you stole my sleep
Even my dreams you chose to keep
To share them with you is somewhat new
Although my dreams are all about you

The memories we share, for me are a treasure
These feelings to share is only a pleasure
I am glad that you get to listen to my thoughts
I am glad you know that love is a positive force

A love that we can share not only in a dream
A love in reality that flows like a stream
A love embedded deep inside my heart
A love that will spark this romance to start

I hope that you like these dreams of mine
I hope that they touch your heart so fine
I hope that you get to show me how you feel
I hope that this love with a kiss you will seal.

Love Burns

Love burns deep, love burns true
Love leaves you breathless and unsure of what to do
Love makes you pine for hours on end
Love makes you weak to those who do not comprehend

Love makes life worth living
It challenges the heart to be forgiving
Love makes you want to reach for every star
It allows you the freedom to be who you are

No matter the situation you find yourself in
Think of those special feelings deep within
Listen to your heart and let love shine
Open your heart and forever be mine.

Love

Love is a feeling that is hard to explain
It can knock you down like a runaway train
Love gives you the wings you need to fly
Soaring above the clouds, high up in the sky

Love gives you the bravery to embrace any fear
It gives you more strength when your loved one is near
Love gives you hope when you stumble and fall
Love gives you the wisdom to stand up tall

Love lifts you up when you lose all hope
Love gives you the confidence and allows you to cope
With whatever the world chooses to throw your way
Love is the thing that makes you want to fight back and stay.

My Love, My Life And My All

Thank you for being my shining light
For brightening up even the darkest of night
Thank you for being my pillar of strength
For helping me maintain my common sense

Thank you for holding my heart so close
For giving me the pleasure to cherish you the most
Thank you for always having my back
For helping me always stay on track

To cherish this special treasure of mine
And to tell you that I see you as no less than divine
You will always be my love, my life and my all
And I will forever be at your beck and call.

Only For You

Only for you, I can climb the greatest of heights
Only for you, I can find beauty in all the sights
Only for you, I can swim the vast seas
Only for you, I could walk a mile on my knees

Only for you, I would jump out of a moving plane
Only for you, I would never want to complain
Only for you, I would take on any dare
Only for you, I would lay my heart bare

Only for you, I would walk barefoot on fire
Only for you, I will embrace my deepest desire
Only for you, I can take on the Heavens above
Only for you, I would sacrifice all my love.

Proposal

I never thought this dream would come true
When I would go down on one knee yo propose to you
The road we travelled at times was rough
But our hearts have proved that our love was tough.

Words will always be on my lips for you
To allow my heart to stay forever true
These words are what made me smile all day
For these words to you I only dreamt I would say

As I slowly get down on my knee
Her heart melts when she locks eyes with me
Holding out a ring I begin to say, "Will you stand by my side?"
"Will you marry me and be my bride?"

Some Say Love

Some say that love is a beautiful thing
It feels like a magical shower in spring
Some say that love can make you weak at the knees
And at times like you are sailing the seas

Some say that love can make you float in the air
To give you the answers to all of your prayers
Some say that love is a wicked game
In which you can never be the same

Some say that love is a dream come true
And that it brings endless magic to everything you do
Some say that love makes life worth living
For which your heart is truly worth giving.

Tell Me You Love Me

Tell me you love me and tell me it is true
So that I may share my heart with you
Tell me that your feelings for me are real
So that I may show you how I feel

Tell me how special you want your life to be
So that I can show you how much you mean to me
Tell me what brings joy to your heart
And I will show you that nothing can keep us apart

Tell me what your heart loves the most
And about you, to the world I will boast
Tell me you love me and tell me it is true
And I will show you that I love you too.

The Moon Adds Light

The moon adds light to the nights sky
Sending lovers emotions on a new high
Setting the tone for a romantic night
Where lovers enjoy meals by candlelight

Such great energy and vibe the moment does bring
That a queen shall be asked to dance by her king
Melodies of love that will forever play
Whilst deep in your heart she will forever stay

To stay in her thoughts forever, if only he could
To show her his love he definitely would
To ease her mind of how he feels about her
A love that grows deeper, year by year

Embracing the world with his love by his side
Embracing the journey and even the ride
Believe in each other and make good on what you say
Profess your love for each other each and every day.

The Special One

There is that special moment in time
When you are blessed with a partner in crime
One who makes your life feel complete
One whose love does not lie, steal or cheat

They help you see the world as beautiful
And for their love, you are eternally grateful
For all the time you spend together
Leaves joy in your heart that will stay forever

The strength you share when two become one
Is a strength that makes nothing impossible to overcome
Hold her close and never let her go
Hold her close and let your love for her flow

Tell her truly how you feel within
Tell her openly what her love will bring
How full your journey and pleasures be
Tell her how special she is to thee.

Walk Beside Me

Walk beside me and hold my hand
And forever beside you, I will stand
Keep me close and keep me near
From my love, you have nothing to fear

Beside you forever is where I promise to stay
No matter what life may throw our way
Take in this moment where we get to dance
Look at our love and be thankful for this chance

I will fill your mornings with the brightest of beams
And at night I will help you capture your dreams
So walk beside me and hold my hand
And beside you forever is where I promise to stand.

When I Close My Eyes

When I close my eyes, I see a vision of you
Settling in like the morning dew
Oh, what freshness of hope you bring
Oh, what songs my heart starts to sing

A vision of beauty that captures all thought
This beauty in abundance cannot be bought
I dare not want to open these eyes
I dare not want to hear my hearts cries

I want your beauty in my mind to stay
To challenge my heart in every way
Stay locked in my thoughts, to never depart
To dance to the tunes that come from my heart

If only you could see what you have done to me
Is there anything else my eyes will get to see?
I will treasure these moments when I close my eyes
The visions of you are my most treasured prize.

DREAMS OF THE SOUL

A Beautiful Day

A beautiful day starts with a positive thought
It is filled with love that the Heavens have brought
You are a breath of fresh air and a welcome change
That breathes new life into a world so strange

A beautiful day is what we all search for
So, open your hearts and steer darkness out the door
You bring new hope for one and all
And we openly embrace your heartfelt call

A beautiful day is a welcomed sight
As the sun shines down with all its might
You bring to us so much tranquility
That allows us to get back some of our sanity
So, let us be thankful for this beautiful day
And embrace the beauty that it brings our way.

A New Adventure

Some say that broken hearts may never mend
And the painful memories may never end
Whilst tears that were shed will never dry
And the love that was shared, was no more than a lie

These are the thoughts of one that is bitter
A pure heart that one day will wither
For life is not only a bed of roses
Nor does life cease when one door closes

Pick up your head and dust off your pain
For the world needs exploring and for you to begin again
Let not the past be in control of your future
Find love within and go out on a new adventure.

A Sense Of Growth

As the cool wind blows the leaves around
Some stay strong whilst some fall to the ground
The fallen leaves will soon wither and die
Yet they still supply nourishment to the earth where they lie

So, if ever you find your heart in pain
Remember that happiness is born again
To fill your life with strength in abundance
To remind your heart of its second chance

So never look back and feel that you are lost
For life goes on no matter the cost
Embrace the lessons that we learn whilst we grow
Make them work in unison like an arrow let loos from a bow.

A World Of Pain

A world of pain, a world filled with tears
Where the people live their lives filled with fears
A virus has taken over all our light
A virus that can strike down those with the strongest of might

We hear the sad news of loved ones lost
A plea to all, to work together at all cost
To save humanity during this difficult phase
Stay safe, keep your distance, there are various ways

The rules are simple to save one and all
Put on your mask and sanitize, for even the strong will fall
Take heed of this virus, take heed my dear friend
Protect yourself and save your loved ones from a bitter end.

Burning Eyes

Sleep burns like fire in my eyes
Yet no one hears my silent cries
Sleepless nights do I have to bare
Alone in my room, at the ceiling I stare

Why am I to endure all of this
Will I ever get a night of sleeping bliss?
Thoughts run wild through my mind
I hope that thoughts of peace I can find

Will I ever get to understand this plight of mine?
Or will I be able to find a night divine?
For these burning eyes deserve some rest
and my aching heart needs to be refreshed

Broken Hearts

Broken hearts take time to heal
Broken hearts come with a pain only the host can feel
From the loss that they must endure
Which they fear has no cure

Time is something that teaches us all
From painful memories, love can still call
Love is the glue to mend a broken heart
To give life back its joy and allow pain to depart

Never lose hope, no matter how bad you may feel
Remember that happiness comes from what you decide is real
Life is such that the heart stays strong
Within you no sadness can belong.

Challenge The Norm

If wise men say that only fools rush love
Would it still count as a blessing straight from above?
If it is true that your first love never dies
When they walk away, does their heart ever cry?

If you love someone you should set them free
Should you then walk away and leave them be?
And if broken hearts can never truly mend
Should you live in pain until the very end?

Is it not fear that drives lovers apart?
All because they are afraid of a broken heart
Open your heart and challenge the norm
Be brave, stand up tall and take on the storm.

Do You Remember?

Do you remember the time that you brought her flowers?
And how her smile had lingered for hours?
Do you remember when you used to get lost in those eyes?
Hours would go by before you would even realize

Do you remember how you would hold her hand?
And take her to places that were not so grand
Do you remember the way she made you feel?
And when you were with her, how her actions were real

As time passes by, we start to take things for granted
And all we do is focus on what we wanted
The joy that we shared can never be measured
And those are the memories that should be treasured
So take some time to remember the old ways
Let us make time to relive those wonderful days.

Echoes Of Silence

Echoes of silence filled up the night
As I sat all alone under the beautiful moonlight
I looked up at a sky that was filled with stars
When suddenly the silence was broken by sounds from afar

I was no longer alone embracing the night
And even the silence seemed to have suddenly taken flight
In the blink of an eye my loneliness was gone
And in its place a new energy was born

I opened my ears to the sounds around me
I opened my eyes to all the sights I could see
Echoes of silence I can no longer find
For the beauty around me has filled up my mind.

I Thanked My God

I woke up this morning to face a new day
Words freely escaped me as I started to pray
I thanked my God for what I could see
A beautiful sunrise and birds roaming free

For the breath of fresh air that I felt on my face
For the movement of people outside my place
For strength in abundance to take on this day
To face new challenges that come my way

I prayed to my God to ease all of our pain
To give us a chance to build our lives again
To give strength to those that mourn
And from the ashes may new life be born

But most of all I thanked him for life
For giving us the courage to stand strong in strife
To comfort those in pain and sorrow
And to give them hope of a better tomorrow.

If I Turn To You

If I turn to you just to talk
Would you listen to me or turn and walk?
If I turn to you when I need a friend
Would you stand beside me till the end?

If I turn to you when I am sad
Would you be the comfort I never had?
If I turn to you to show me the way
Would you come along and beside me stay?

If I turn to you on a cold winters night
Would you sit with me by the fires light?
If I turn to you to say goodbye
Would you hold me close and never cry?

Is There Another Love Out There For Me?

Is there another love out there for me?
Will I ever be able to set this broken heart free?
I find myself wondering about my life
Will I be another man's wife?

I lost all hope when I lost my true love
He was called to join the Angels up above
Will I be free from this pain of losing you?
Will I find another whose love is so true?

I can smile with joy from the love we had
It helps me go on even though I am sad
It gives me the strength to face another day
To look at the Heavens and thankfully pray

I hear his voice deep in my heart
I feel his love even though we are apart
I long for his touch, his gentle embrace
The feel of his breath as he kisses my face

Will I be able to move on with my life?
Will I be another man's wife?
I wish there were answers for this heart of mine
I wish you could tell me that I will be just fine.

Journey Of Life

The journey of life can be a magical ride
If you have someone special by your side
Someone to hold when you are feeling down
Someone to save you, should you start to drown

Someone to lean on should you feel weak
Someone to celebrate your winning streak
But most of all a pillar of hope
That shoulders all your troubles to help you cope

A friend who is willing to share your chores
Who is not afraid to show you your flaws
And when you need to be held at night
With gentle hands they will hold you tight

The love they have is deep and pure
For all your heartaches they are the cure
To make you smile when you are sad
Or stand close by when you are mad
To show you how special life can be
To shower your mind with love so free.

Let Your Love Shine

Let your love shine from deep within
Let your loved ones feel the joy that you bring
Let the sweetest of thoughts come out to play
And know that your sorrows are not here to stay

Let your happiness fall all around us like rain
Let your laughter slowly remove all our pain
Let your spirit be free to come out of its trance
And let out your heart to sing and dance

Let your love shine bright like the stars at night
Let your eyes take in this beautiful sight
Let your loved ones know how much they mean to you
And let your heart stay strong in all that you do.

Life Is A Breeze

Life is a breeze that is carried on the wings of a dove
Tread safely wherever you may be, my love
For life is fragile and needs a lot of tender care
So be mindful when you are out there

Time slips away but memories will remain
Use them wisely and keep your heart out of pain
Think of the things that you would love to do
And put in the effort to make them come true

Open your heart and fill it with hope
Stay strong on your feet as you conquer the slope
For life is a breeze that is gentle yet strong
Trust in yourself and you can never go wrong.

Love Is A Feeling

Love is in the air, so they say
Love is a feeling we share every day
Love is found in all that we do
Love is a feeling that is forever true

Love holds us captive and love sets us free
Love holds us firm, through the roughest sea
Love gave us life through the passions of birth
Love gives us the freedom to roam the earth

Love makes us crazy and walk in a daze
Love gives us comfort when we are stuck in a maze
Love keeps us sane when we are falling apart
Love is the glue to mend every broken heart

So, take comfort in this feeling called love
Take comfort and enjoy what is sent from above
No matter what you say and even what you do
Love is a feeling that will stay forever true.

New Dreams

When we close our eyes and start to sleep
We lose all senses that when awake we keep
All our inhibitions have suddenly gone
And in its place new dreams are born

How peaceful is the look our faces tend to hold
For in our dreams we dare to be bold
We can challenge the strong to any duel
We can mine the earth for the most precious of jewel

We find the courage to shout out with joy
We embrace the beauty without being coy
The things we can do when we close our eyes
We may still be in bed but oh, how we rise.

Stars

The day is over when the stars come out to play
We look at the Heavens as the sun fades away
The day we lived is now in the past
Treasure the memories as the shadows are cast

The warmth of the sunshine that embraced us all
Filled our lives with its rise and fall
As the night slowly starts to take its place
The day has finally left without a trace

I lay on the grass and look up at the sky
I stare in amazement as a plane goes by
How awesome it would be to dance among the stars
Or even to travel out to Mars

Endless thoughts fill up our mind
Use them wisely or you will be left behind
I embraced the beauty of a cloudless sky
Filled with stars in the Heavens way up high.

Stolen Moments

Stolen moments are all that we share
Stolen moments captured together out there
For time is something that is never on our side
Time is as constant as a changing tide

The life we live is not a simple one
Whilst the feelings we share bring so much fun
It allows us the freedom to challenge the norm
To stand firm together and face the storm.

If only we had the freedom to explore
To never settle but always crave more
For stolen moments is all that we share
Stolen moments captured together out there.

The Beauty Within

The beauty of a person lies in not what you see
For beauty from within is thoughtful and free
Pure beauty from within makes you stand out
The emotions that are shown leave no room for doubt

The look in their eyes melts any resistance
And removes any fear from your heart of loves existence
As you struggle to find the words to say
Know that your beauty within speaks in its own way

For it is filled with stories of love and strife
It gives you the carefree nature to enjoy your life
When you are free to share what you feel
The beauty within can make your dreams become real.

The Journey

Life is not just about the journey you take
It is also about the people you meet and
memories you make
Some are bad and lessons of life are learnt
And at other times even the strong will get burnt

There is also a lot of good that comes along
This helps you see who and what does belong
The good makes your life better and brighter
And even helps make your burdens lighter

The journey begins when you step out there
And find the one with whom you can freely share
Time and emotions from deep within
Cherish the journey and let life begin.

The Sun Goes Down

The sun goes down at the end of the day
This is the reality come what may
The darkness follows as the sun hides its face
Whilst the stars come out to brighten up the place

Open your eyes and envision your dream
Savor the moment as scary as it may seem
Such are the dreams that fill our mind
Open them up for the world to find

Remember that dreams are ours to share
To show our loved ones how much we care
The choices we make include them all
For they will be there to catch us if ever we fall

Treasure the moments we make come true
Cherish the memories and all that we do
Today is here for us to celebrate
Tomorrow will come, we just have to wait.

Trying Times

Another year has passed us by
A year filled with sadness that I cannot deny
Lives were lost but not in war
From a common enemy both near and far

A year filled with sadness that made us all cry
A year where thousands watched their loved ones die
A year where we all lived in the greatest of fear
Whilst a faceless killer took all that was dear

The year is over, but the danger is not
Think of the destruction and protect whatever you have got
For trying times is where we currently are
So, take precautions and care, whether near or far.

Twist Of Fate

A change of life from a twist of fate
Can burden your shoulders with extra weight
Feelings that run wild and out of control
Where the smallest of emotions can harm your soul

Which emotions would you want to set free?
A heartless person would you want to be?
Think of the life that you would lead
Think of the people that you would need

Never look down, never lose hope
No matter your fate, with life you can cope
Bring out the smiles and change your state
Make it memorable, this twist of fate

You may never forget but remember to forgive
Let only love within you live
Release your anger and open your heart
And that is when your life will truly start.

When The Sun Comes Out

When the sun comes out and the night is done
We embrace new life, we search for fun
With the dawn of time and the journeys to come
We open our eyes to what we have become

Chase for the stars or even the moon
Chase for your dreams but do it soon
The sun will set and rise again
Time will pass but only memories will remain

Embrace the day and embrace your life too
Challenge the norm with everything you do
Never look back or regret your past
Make the most of life and go out with a blast

Words of wisdom we take to heart
Take heed of these words and make a fresh start
The journey of life is a dream come true
Seize the day and let it embrace you.

DREAMS OF THE EARTH

As The Winds Blow

As the winds blow through the trees all around
I watch as the leaves flutter and fall to the ground
I watch in awe as nature does its thing
I watch in awe for it is autumn and not spring

This is the time when leaves choose to die
For the changing of season means they have to say goodbye
How does this climate know when to change?
It won't be permanent but isn't it strange?

As the sun begins to rise and the moon is set to depart
Hours later the stars will return to play its part
Chasing the sun and its abundance of light
So that once more from day, it turns to night

How often do we stop to take all this in?
How often would we say, "Let nature take this win"?
So, take heed of your surroundings when you are out
Enjoy natures beauty, dance, sing and shout.

Freedom

The wind blew her hair onto my face
Whilst she cantered along with such grace
I held my breath as she fastened her stride
For the excitement of freedom she dared not hide
I loosened the reigns and let her go
I was not afraid for I trusted her so

Up to the hills she galloped on gracefully
With me on her back going along willingly
It was my first time, but I felt so at ease
So, I allowed this horse to do as she would please
At last when we reached the top of the hill
The world around me seemed so still

The sight before me left me in awe
For the sight before me shook my very core
Right in front of me lay vast lands
So pure and untouched by human hands
And what beautiful flowers scattered all around
A paradise of freedom, a treasure I have found.

I Am Thankful

As I lie here all alone in the quiet of the night
I enjoy every moment as I drown out the light
I am thankful for the peace that surrounds me
I am thankful as I get to set my thoughts free

Free to enjoy the serenity all around
Feeling inspired and profound
I open my eyes and look up at the sky
I am thankful for the moonlight that catches my eye

As the light from the moon brightens this place
I am thankful for the feel of Heavens grace
It fills my heart with tranquility and peace
As I lay here in awe and my worries start to cease.

I Believe

I believe that everything in life happens for a reason
And people may enter your life like the changing of a season
They bring about feelings that are new
They challenge you in all that you choose to do

Welcome this chance to make a change
Never look back, even though it may seem strange
The winds will blow throughout the year
And based on the seasons you need not fear

The summer season is warm and bright
Whilst the winter winds give chills through the night
No matter the season, we will find ways to live
Our bond with nature is such, we always thrive
no matter what it may give.

I Look Up At The Stars

I look up at the stars in the sky so bright
And I can only applaud this beautiful sight
Not a single cloud could be seen up high
Not a single blemish on this beautiful sky

The stars add light to this cloudless night
It covers the earth with its natural light
People are abuzz, moving to and fro
Whilst I just sit by idly, watching them go

I hear the sounds of the birds chirping tonight
Yet their physical presence is out of sight
This adds a special gift from nature
Something my mind will dearly treasure.

I Searched For The Moon

I look up at the sky in search of the moon
Where are you hiding? Please come out soon
For the sky is dark and looks so sad
Any glimmer of light will make me so glad

This place is dark and feels kind of creepy
Although it is night I am not yet sleepy
I look around for something to do
But with the place being in darkness, I have no clue

I search for the moon in the sky once again
And to my joy, my search was not in vain
I spot the moon as the clouds move along
High above the earth in the sky where it does belong.

I See

I see trees and flowers all around me
I see birds and butterflies roaming free
I see little children running past
Enjoying nature and having a blast

I see the waves crashing along the shore
I see divers take the plunge, excited
although unsure
I see mothers and fathers holding hands
I see children playing joyfully in the sand

How pleasant a feeling to see children play
They enjoy Mother Nature in every single way
If only we all could see through their eyes
How much more respectful we would be to nature's cries.

Nature My Friends

Another beautiful sunrise has come my way
Yet the sky is filled with clouds today
As the sun begins to warm up the earth
The birds begin to forage in the dirt

Nature my friends is awesome to see
All living organisms just roaming free
They embrace the light with their special song
They go out in search as though nothing is wrong

If only the humans that inhabit the land
Pay homage to nature and their magical band
Would enjoy the sounds that they share with all
With endless thanks to creatures big and small.

New Day

A beautiful new day begins at the break of dawn
When the rising sun creates a brand-new morn
We open our eyes and take in this sight
Whilst the rising sun burns ever so bright

With the start of a new day comes new hope
Whilst with yesterday's troubles we are able to cope
A new day teaches us of better things to come
A new day gives another chance for our fears to be overcome

Stay positive in mind and strong at heart
For with each new day, you will have to play your part
So, embrace the journey you find yourself on
Embrace the new day with the rising of the sun.

Spring Time

As winter passes and spring is in the air
It is Mother Nature's special time of the year
When flowers bloom and brighten the earth
The world's natural beauty has a rebirth.

What an awesome sight that fills our lives
Whilst all around us nature comes alive
The earth looks fresh and green
Whilst the air is crisp and clean.

As flowers bloom and birds start to sing
Great joy and happiness to our hearts it does bring
So open your eyes and take in this beauty
Embrace the season, make it your duty
Thank you, Lord, for this amazing treasure
Thank you for blessing us with all this pleasure.

Summer Sun

As the Heavens shower us with a beautiful new day
And the summer sun brightens up our way
Let us embrace the moment as we open our eyes
Let us be thankful for the birds that takes to the skies

The sun looks down and blesses us all
And every being nature answers its call
The rays are strong and infinitely bright
And to the entire world it adds so much light

As the summer sun looks down from above
Embrace its beauty and its love
Absorb the warmth that is given today
Thank the Lord for giving us another beautiful day.

Summer's Rain

As the rain falls gently on a warm summer's day
I look at the Heavens and silently I pray
The coolness it brings as it pours down from above
The purest of blessings rain down with love

I run out in the yard to dance in the rain
Like a child would do whilst his mum would complain
I dance for joy as I watch the rain fall
I dance as though I have no worries at all

As the rain falls and cools the earth down
I do not bother if anyone is around
For the summer's rain has finally appeared
And from our minds all doubt is cleared

For the earth was dry from taking in this sun
Summer was here but the heat was no fun
So, thank you Lord, for sending the summer's rain
Oh, thank you Lord, for relieving the earth's pain.

Warmth Of The Sun

I stepped out of the house and what did I see?
This beautiful sun shining down on me
I felt its warmth upon my face
As I turned my eyes and stared into space.

I started to wonder whilst standing there
How amazing the sight of the birds in the air
How awesome it would be if I had their view
How awesome a dream if only it came true.

As I stood with my feet planted firmly in the ground
I smiled at the crazy thoughts that my mind had found
I smiled as I felt the warmth of the sun
I will cherish this moment before the day is done.

DREAMS OF GOOD TIMES

A Rose

The flower of love is called a rose
Its majestic beauty can be used to propose
Red roses signify true love, desire and romance
It can create waves with just one glance

Yellow roses signify care, joy and friendship
Which in time can lead to a beautiful relationship
For a strong bond starts with being good friends
And then it blossoms into love that we pray never ends

Orange roses signify enthusiasm, energy and desire
Once started, it can be loves eternal fire
That burns bright in the hearts of those in love
Which fit together, hand in glove

White roses signify purity and innocence
It will give true love all the confidence
So, remember to reveal all that is in your heart
So that your journey in life is true from the start.

Birthday Wishes

Birthday wishes I send to you
May all your wishes come true
You are an Angel on Earth, sent here from Heaven
Whose inner beauty is shown through every expression

I wish you the best as you start your day
May you be spoilt in every way
May your heart's desires be fulfilled
May only tears of joy be spilled

Arise my beauty, for the day has come
When a bundle of joy became a blessing to your mum
As you arise to celebrate this day
Make the most of it and have an awesome birthday.

Doom

I heard his voice clearly across the room
My heart yelled out, "Here comes doom"
No matter what he had to say
Far from him I would run away

Why he troubles me I do not know
Or why my only wish is for him to go
My emotions show me a sign of danger
But if I run, would it be a game changer?

How can I send my thoughts to him?
To make him understand is all but grim
The lights are on yet no one is home
Please help my heart not turn to stone.

Drunken State

Beauty is sometimes defined by whoever holds the drink
The bolder they become, the less they think
They can promise you the sun, the moon, or the world
Woo you tirelessly now but tomorrow will not remember a word

They will express their emotions in their drunken state
Even impress you endlessly about their faith
They can belt out tunes, thinking they sound good
But they can also brighten up the dullest of mood

But once they fully come to their senses
Watch how they begin to prepare their defences

Deny all the promises that they have made
And like a shadow they will eventually fade
Beware of promises made by one in a drunken state
For they will be forgotten once they are sober, make no mistake.

Eyes Wide Shut

As dawn approaches and my sleep begins to break
My eyes are still closed yet I am wide awake
I take heed of the thoughts playing around in my head
And smile to myself as I lay there in bed

Should I awake and take on this day?
And embrace the things that will come my way
My mind is at ease whilst I remain in this state
It wishes to vegetate further and wake up late

With my eyes wide shut I start to dream
Carried away by a calm current, like a flower in a stream
Whilst I am enjoying the tranquility of my rest
I cannot help but think that this my friends, is laziness at its best.

Halloween

It was a beautiful night when the moon came out to play
The stars shone bright and chased the clouds away
Rapturous laughter in the distance could be heard
Where the joyous festivities had occurred

Children dressed up like monsters and skipped to a beat
Going from house to house shouting, "Trick or Treat?"
Adults played like children whilst walking the streets
Carrying buckets filled to the brim with sweets

What an amazing experience for all that were there
I could not help but to stop and stare
Watching a daughter with her mom and a dad with his son
Purely mesmerized at both young and old
having so much of fun.

ABOUT THE AUTHOR

Mervin M. Francis releases his second poetry anthology. Mervin hails from the North Coast of Kwa-Zulu Natal, South Africa. Currently in a career with Toyota SA, Mervin still continues to write poetry on the side. The poetry is written to express the joy of the world around him . He continues to publish his work so that he may share it with the rest of the world.

www.ingramcontent.com/pod-product-compliance
Lightning Source LLC
Chambersburg PA
CBHW042047290426
44109CB00006B/140